THE MONSTER
IN THE HALL

by David Greig

*Part of the British Council Edinburgh Showcase 2011:
August 22-27*

Supported by

The Monster in the Hall was commissioned by the Citizens Theatre in 2009, as a TAG production. TAG produces the Citizens Theatre's work for children and young people, enjoyed by all ages.

The production was first produced in association with Arts and Theatres Trust Fife and was premiered at Kirkland High School and Community College, Fife, on 23 September 2010, then toured to community centres and small-scale venues across Scotland before culminating in a two-week run at the Citizens Theatre. In 2011, the play was re-staged at the Traverse Theatre as part of the Edinburgh Festival Fringe.

What did you think?

There are lots of ways to send us your feedback

Rate the show you've just seen
You can leave your comments and ratings on our website show pages

Text your feedback
Text the word CITZ and your comment to 61211 (normal text charge applies)

Email us at info@citz.co.uk

Write to us at Citizens Theatre, 119 Gorbals St, Glasgow G5 9DS

Connect with us

citz.co.uk
facebook.com/citizenstheatre
twitter.com/citizenstheatre
flickr.com/citizenstheatre
citizenstheatre.blogspot.com

The Monster in the Hall
by David Greig

Cast

Lawrence Lofthouse	**David Carlyle**
Hugh Macatarsney	**Keith Macpherson**
Ms Agnetha Bergholm /	
Mrs Linda Underhill	**Beth Marshall**
Duck Macatarsney	**Gemma McElhinney**

Production Team

Director	**Guy Hollands**
Music & Sound Design	**Nigel Dunn & Stephen Wright**
Choreographer	**Andrew Panton**
Production Manager	**Laura Smith**
Costume Design	**Elaine G. Coyle**
Assistant Director 2011 Tour	**Amanda Gaughan**
Assistant Director 2010 Tour	**Howie Reeve**

Special thanks to

All the staff at the Citizens Theatre, Frank Chinn and all at Arts and Theatres Trust Fife, Nina Collins at Fife Young Carers, Neil Murray at National Theatre of Scotland, Roddy Lambie, Ronnie Ross and the staff and students of Kirkland High School and Community College, George Drennan, Ian Piercy, Alan Wilkins and the RSAMD.

The play contains swearing and some sexual references.
Recommended for 14 +

 The Citizens company was founded in 1943 by James Bridie, and the Citizens Theatre was permanently established in 1945. Since then it has been one of Scotland's flagship producing theatres.

The Citizens has a distinguished history that continues today, presenting a world-class repertoire based on British and foreign classics, contemporary plays and new writing. We provide high quality main house and studio productions, theatre for children and young people, a regular programme of theatre on tour, two non-professional acting companies, drama classes for children and adults and a pioneering range of creative participatory projects delivered by Learning and TAG. We have extensive backstage workshop facilities and make our own sets and costumes.

The Citizens Theatre is firmly rooted in its local community and we place a special emphasis on work with children, young people and socially excluded adults. We believe in placing arts, culture and creativity at the heart of learning and provide opportunities at the theatre and in communities and schools across Scotland, for young people and adults to engage with drama.

Artistic Director   **Dominic Hill**
Adminstrative Director   **Anna Stapleton**
Chairman   **Murray Buchanan**
Vice Chair   **Professor Adrienne Scullion**

Citizens Theatre
119 Gorbals St
Glasgow G5 9DS

Registered Company no: SCO 22513

Registered Charity no: SCO 01337

+44 (0) 141 429 5561
citz.co.uk

Biographies

David Carlyle   *Lawrence Lofthouse*
David graduated from Rose Bruford College in 2010. David recently appeared in *Dead Heavy Fantastic* (Liverpool Everyman) and *Caledonia* (NTS). His theatre credits whilst training include *Ringing in Your Ears* (Rose Bruford / Royal Court Young Writers), *The Wonderful World of Dissocia*, *Philistines*, *The White Devil*, *Celebration*, *Party Time* and *Hedda Gabler* (Rose Bruford). TV credits include *Lip Service* (BBC). David represented Rose Bruford in the 2010 Sam Wannamaker Festival at Shakespeare's Globe Theatre, playing Flomenio in *The White Devil*.

Nigel Dunn   *Music & Sound Design*
Nigel studied at Perth College and is actually qualified to 'Rock!'. He has worked as a musical director for many shows during the past ten years at venues ranging from the London National and the Millennium Dome to the Traverse and Cumbernauld Theatres. He has released singles and albums with various bands. He also works as a producer and has film and TV soundtrack credits under the guise of Moonglass Music.

Guy Hollands   *Director*
Guy's theatre credits include *The Crucible* (TAG / NTS), *Meep and Moop*, *Museum of Dreams*, *Liar*, *Yellow Moon*, *Ice Cream Dreams*, *The Visit*, *A Taste of Honey*, *Knives in Hens* and *The Birthday Party* (TAG), *Beauty and the Beast*, *Othello*, *Hamlet*, *The Wizard of Oz*, *Waiting for Godot*, *Nightingale and Chase*, *The Fever*, *Night School* and *The Caretaker* (Citizens Theatre), *Woyzeck* (Royal Lyceum, Edinburgh / KtC), *Pinocchio* (Visible Fictions), *Earball* (Tosg) and *Factory Girls* (7:84). He will direct *Hansel and Gretel* for the Citizens Theatre in December 2011.

Beth Marshall   *Ms Agnetha Bergholm / Mrs Linda Underhill*
Beth has worked extensively in repertory theatre including a year with Dundee Rep Ensemble, four seasons with Mull Theatre and six seasons with Bard in the Botanics. Other credits include *Six Black Candles* (Goldfish Theatre), *A Christmas Carol* (NTS), *Peter Pan* (Citizens Theatre), *Tam O'Shanter* (Perth Theatre), *Brave* (Communicado / Sounds of Progress), *The Night Before Christmas* (Belgrade Theatre), *The Bondagers* (Byre Theatre), *Fergus Lamont* (Communicado / Perth Theatre) and *Yellow Moon* (TAG).

Gemma McElhinney   *Duck Macatarsney*
Gemma trained at Queen Margaret University. Her theatre credits include *Beauty and the Beast*, *Don't Start Me!* (Citizens Theatre), *10,000 Meters Deep* (Oran Mor), *Peer Gynt* (Dundee Rep / NTS), *Quelques Fleurs*, *Who's Afraid of Virginia Woolf?*, *Beauty and the Beast*, *Mother Courage* (Dundee Rep), *Bye Bye Birdie* (Brunton Theatre), *Trojan Women*, *Medea*, *Time and the Conways* and *The Tempest* (Queen Margaret University). Film credits include *Meta* (Matt Cameron). Gemma was nominated for Best Female Performance at the Critics Awards for Theatre in Scotland 2011.

Keith Macpherson   *Hugh Macatarsney*

Keith's theatre credits include *A Christmas Carol* (Cumbernauld Theatre), *Mother Courage*, *Clutter Keeps Company* (Birds of Paradise), *4:48 Psychosis* (SweetScar / Tramway / Cumbernauld), *The Wizard of Oz*, *Waiting for Godot*, *Peter Pan*, *Desire Under the Elms* (Citizens Theatre), *Yellow Moon* (TAG), *Faust* (Royal Lyceum, Edinburgh), *Factory Girls* (7:84), *The Lost Child* (Minerva Theatre), *Invisible Man* (Vanishing Point), *Brave* (Communicado), *Decky Does a Bronco* (Grid Iron / Almeida), *Timeless* (Suspect Culture), *Macbeth* (Chester Gateway) and *Cigarettes and Chocolate* (KtC).

Andrew Panton   *Choreographer*

Andrew's theatre credits include *Spring Awakening* (Director / Choreographer, Edinburgh Fringe), *Sweeney Todd* (Movement Director, Dundee Rep), *Honk!* (Director / Choreographer, Royal & Derngate), *Black Watch* (Assistant Director, National Theatre of Scotland), *The Magnets – Gobsmacked* (Director / Choreographer, Roundhouse), (*Sunset Song* (Movement Director, Scottish Tour), *A Drop in the Ocean* (Director, Oran Mor), *The Wizard of Oz* (Co-Director, Citizens Theatre), *A Sheep Called Skye* (Director, NTS), *Sundowe* (Movement Director, Eden Court Theatre / Cameron Mackintosh), *Hamlet* (Composer, Citizens Theatre), *The Wonderful World of Dissocia* (Vocal / Movement Coach, NTS), *Gorgeous Avatar* (Movement Director, Traverse Theatre). TV credits include *Tonight's the Night* with John Barrowman, Commercials for *S1 Jobs*, *Haka, Grolsch* and Irn Bru's tribute to *High School Musical*.

The Monster in the Hall

David Greig was born in Edinburgh. His plays include
Europe, *The Architect*, *The Speculator*, *The Cosmonaut's
Last Message to the Woman He Once Loved in the
Former Soviet Union*, *Outlying Islands*, *San Diego*,
Pyrenees, *The American Pilot*, *Yellow Moon: The Ballad
of Leila and Lee*, *Damascus*, *Midsummer* (*a Play with
Songs*), *Dunsinane* and *The Strange Undoing of Prudencia
Hart*. In 1990 he co-founded Suspect Culture to produce
collaborative, experimental theatre work. His translations
and adaptations include Camus's *Caligula*, Euripides'
The Bacchae, Strindberg's *Creditors* and *Peter Pan*.

DAVID GREIG

The Monster in the Hall

faber and faber

First published in 2011
by Faber and Faber Limited
74–77 Great Russell Street, London WC1B 3DA

Typeset by Country Setting, Kingsdown, Kent CT14 8ES
Printed and bound by CPI Group (UK) Ltd, Croydon, CR0 4YY

A CIP record for this book
is available from the British Library

ISBN 978–0–571–28287–6

2 4 6 8 10 9 7 5 3 1

Characters

Duck Macatarsney

Hugh Macatarsney

Lawrence Lofthouse

Ms Agnetha Bergholm

Mrs Linda Underhill

Is this on?

　Cough.

Testing –

Testing –

Testing –

Testing –

1 –

2 –

3 –

Go!

*

　Thunder.

　Rain.

　Motorcycle screech.

No no no no no no no no!

　Motorcycle crash.

*

Hello

I'm Keith

I'm Beth

I'm David

And I'm Gemma

And together we are

The Fabulous Duckettes.

We're here today

To tell you the true story

Of Duck Macatarsney

A teenage girl from the little Scottish town of
Kirkcaldy.

It's a story of pain

(Pain)

Misery

(Misery)

Embarrassment and

Shame.

It's a story with sex

(Sex)

Death, humiliation and catastrophe

It's also got a small amount of Socialism.

Socialism?

You won't notice, honestly, it'll be fine.

OK.

It's a tragic but ultimately uplifting tale

Of an ordinary girl

Who looks after her dad in a two-bed flat.

Her mum died in a motorcycle accident when she was only three

Skidded off the road and into a tree.

It was raining.

Just near the turn off to Coaltown of Balgonie.

*

Motorcycle skid.

No no no no no no no.

Motorcycle crash.

*

Duck is short for Ducati,

Her mum's favourite type of bike.

Duck has long brown hair down to the small of her back.

She has a tiny mole on her chin.

She wears big thick glasses.

The sort of girl that if she took off her glasses and shook her hair

It would turn out that she was very very beautiful in a way which had been – until then –

Completely unnoticeable

Unfortunately Duck is very short-sighted

So she never takes her glasses off

And if she ever did

And shook her hair

She would probably accidently hit her head off a wall

And the world would go

Very very blurry.

Duck's the kind of girl who

If she worked part time in a supermarket

Which she does

And one day a famous film director happened to be passing

Three nights a week and all day Saturday

Maybe on his way to St Andrews

Maybe he's making a film

About golf.

Fighting Golf.

Maybe a film director is making a film about Scottish fighting golf and he just suddenly fancies a Crunchie as he goes past Kirkcaldy Asda and so he stops and goes in and –

Crunchie.

And just as Duck passes the honeycombed bar over the barcode reader the film director looks at her and thinks:

She's quite nice

I wonder if she can act.

If she can act maybe she can play the part of the girl's second best friend in the film that I'm making.

I wonder . . .

That'll be seventy-six pence, please.

. . . No. Probably not.

That's the sort of girl Duck is.

So welcome,

Ladies and gentlemen,

Make yourself comfortable

Take warning and enjoy

The story

Of

Duck Macatarsney

And

The Monster in the Hall.

*

Motorcycle screech.

Look out look out look out look out –

   Motorcycle crash.

*

Owwwwwwwww.

Duck?

Ow ow ow ow ow ow ow ow.

Is that you?

Yeah.

What?

Monster.

Oh.

Toe.

Oww.

Cut.

Sorry.

You said you'd tidy.

Sorry.

You should be up.

Sorry.

The lady's coming today.

I know.

Dad?

Yeah.

Are you OK?

Yeah, fine.

Good.

Duck?

Yeah.

Switch the light on, would you?

Why?

*

Why –

Why ay ay ay –
When her dad said, 'Switch the light on.'
Did Duck ask
Why?

*

May
Morning.
The sun rises over Kirkcaldy
Like the headlamp of a giant celestial Harley
Filling the sky
Filling our eyes with light.
Duck Macatarsney opens her eyes
And swings out of bed and thinks
Why?
Why ay ay ay ay ay ay –
Why's it so quiet?
Dad?
Normally he'd be in the kitchen.
Pouring out cornflakes.
Spilling milk everywhere.
But it's all quiet.
Why?

She goes through to the kitchen and her eyes glance from
one corner of mess to another like a tiny elf ballerina

dancing on a stage of crap . . . Ohhh tink . . . An empty pizza box open and with cheese still in it . . . Ooh plink . . . an ashtray full of spliff ends . . . Ooh plunk a pair of Dad's pants tucked half under the oven . . . Oooh tonk socks on the kitchen tabletop where I used them to wipe up spilled lager and oohh plink another pizza box with a bit of pizza still in it and the very faint but nonetheless discernible footprints of a mouse running through the congealed skin of the orange cheese . . . Tink plink plunk tonk . . .

Oh God.

Tee hee.

You again.

Hello, Duck.

What are you doing here?

Why, I am the Fairy of Catastrophe and today I am come to visit ye.

That's no surprise. You're always turning up.

Catastrophe is my name and mischief is my game. Wherever I alight I do turn all lovely things to terrible and today I have alighted here in your kitchen where I do dance about and wave my wand of doom. Tink plink plunk –

But why have you come to my house today, Fairy of Catastrophe?

I have come to your house today because today is the worst possible day I could come to your house.

Why?

Because today is the day the lady is coming to lunch.

. . .

Did you forget?

Aaaaargghhhh!

I knew you'd forget.

Dad! Wake up!
Today's the day the lady's coming.
We've got to get this place tidied up.

But before Duck's eyes can adjust to the light

Her bare foot treads in something soft and squelchy and warm which smells of sweet coconut

Duck jumps away from the coconut poo

But she forgets that she's in the hall

And the hall is where the monster lives

And so she leaps up in the air and when she comes down she lands right on the monster's chain.

Aaaaaaarrrrrrghhhhhhh!

Duck?

Owwwwwwwww!

Is that you?

Yeah.

What?

Monster.

Oh.

Toe.

Oww.

Cut.

Sorry.

You said you'd tidy.

Sorry.

You should be up.

Sorry.

The lady's coming today.

I know.

Dad?

Yeah.

Are you OK?

Yeah, fine.

Good.

Duck?

Yeah.

Switch the light on, would you?

Why?

Why?

Why?

Shhh!

Dad, the light's already on.

*

Motorcycle skid.

Look out look out look out look out –

Motorcycle crash.

*

The lady's name is Mrs Underhill. She's from the
Department of Child Services. She was just wondering if
it would be all right for her to pop round for a visit one
lunchtime?

Pop?

Yes.

Why?

Just to say hello.

Hello?

Just to see how things are.

Things are fine.

I know but –

But what?

It's always good to have a look.

Why?

In case they're not.

What?

Duck, normally you're such a bright alert girl, but these
last few months you've been all over the place. You can't
concentrate. You're tired. There's great big bags under
your eyes.

It's make-up.

It's bags.

I'm channelling Amy Winehouse.

Duck, we found you asleep in the costume trunk.

17

I can explain.

You're just having a rough patch, it's perfectly normal. Sometimes when pupils have a rough patch it's because things are difficult at home. Mrs Underhill's just going to pop round and carry out a basic home assessment so that together we can work out what systems if any we need to put in place to help you.

Systems?

We need to draw up a care plan that we can all sign off on, that's all.

A care plan?

Yes.

What's a care plan?

A care plan is a strategy which aims to work out how best the different care services can work together to help the child.

Right.

What it's not – Duck – is a plan to put you into care.

*

It's a plan to put me into care.

What?

They think we can't cope.

Who?

The Department of Child Services.

Oh.

It's obviously a trick. She wants to come round at lunchtime. Just 'pop' round, she said. 'Pop' and catch us

18

eating crisps is what she meant. She obviously thinks we must live in a pigsty, sit round watching TV all day.

Right.

It's not fair.

But Duck, we do eat crisps and live in a pigsty and sit round watching TV all day.

We still cope.

Do we?

Don't we?

We do.

Totally.

Totally.

Totally.

Totally.

So what are we going to do about the lady?

We're going to show her. We're going to show her how totally we cope. We're going to show her coping like she's never seen it before. After she's visited us she's going to go to training conferences all round the world and show videos of us coping. We're going to rock her coping world. That's what we're going to do.

Yeah.

How are we going to do that?

*

So I'll tell Mrs Underhill it's fine for her to do a home visit on Saturday?

Totally.

Lunchtime OK?

I'll just check my diary. No, right, that's perfect. I mean everything's totally fine so she's wasting her time but – yeah – no – it all sounds really – that's good. I look forward to it. Actually it sounds brilliant. My dad loves a chance to cook.

Cook?

Lunch – we're going to do lunch.

*

Alarm.

May

Morning.

The sun rises over Kirkcaldy like the headlamp of a great celestial Harley filling the sky filling your eyes with light. Duck Macatarsney blinks and stretches and swings her legs out of her bed and under her desk in a single elegant movement –

Then she reaches out her hand to switch off the alarm which today

As every day

Is set for six a.m.

One hour earlier than she needs to be awake

So that Duck steals one peaceful hour to do the thing she enjoys the most in all the world –

Writing.

That's right.

Duck writes.

Duck's writing a novel.

Kind of *Harry Potter* crossed with *Twilight* crossed with *Lord of The Rings*.

The Princess and the Beast.

Loosely autobiographical.

Every morning at six a.m. Duck writes her novel in a WH Smith diary in neat longhand. She draws smiley faces in the vowels and a little elf ballerina dances on top of the i's instead of a dot.

Tink plunk tonk.

One day Duck's novel will be published.

It will win the Booker Prize.

It will be made into a worldwide smash-hit film.

People will interview her for the television

And she will take off her glasses and shake her hair and . . .

But we're getting ahead of ourselves. Duck has not yet opened her eyes – she has as yet just swung her legs from the bed and flopped her very tired upper body on the desk like a dying swan and now she is letting her ears do the waking up for her.

Seagulls.

The low hum of early morning traffic on the A89.

The tick of the clock.

Duck picks up her pen and writes:

Princess Duck looked contentedly out over her kingdom, the mist hung over the green fields of barley, the seagulls hung in the air over the despondent sea, and the sun hung low over the cold stone walls of the castle.

All was normal.

All was well.

Until

Shh, listen

I'm trying to write.

Do you hear that?

I don't hear anything.

Exactly. It's all gone quiet?

Eh?

Normally your dad would be banging about in the kitchen spilling milk.

So.

You should go and look.

I'm trying to write.

In case something's wrong.

OK.

Oh dear, look at the state of the kitchen.

Oh God

Everything everywhere.

It was tidy when I went to bed.

He must have had another pizza.

Four empty cans of beer.

Ashtrays full.

He must have stayed up

On the computer.

He must have stayed up all night doing whatever it is he does when he's on the computer.

Don't think about it.

He'll be in bed.

Owwwwwwwwww.

Duck?

Ow ow ow ow ow ow.

Is that you?

Yeah.

What?

Monster.

Oh.

Toe.

Oww.

Cut.

Sorry.

You said you'd tidy.

Sorry.

You should be up.

Sorry.

The lady's coming today.

I know.

Dad?

Yeah.

Are you OK?

Yeah, fine.

Good.

Duck?

Yeah.

Switch the light on, would you?

Why?

It's dark.

But Dad, the light's already on.

Oh.

What?

I thought so.

Dad?

I think I've gone blind.

Tink plink plunk.

Sorry, Duck.

*

Duckettes perform the theme tune to Mastermind.

*

Your name, please.

Ducati Macatarsney.

Your occupation.

Schoolgirl and novelist.

And your chosen specialised subject.

My dad.

Ducati Macatarsney. you're a novelist, your chosen specialised subject is your dad and your time starts – now!

What is your dad's name?

Duke Macatarsney – Duke of the Bike – aka The Beast.

I need the name on the card.

Hugh?

Correct.

Of which chapter of the Hell's Angels is your father a member?

Bad Boys of the East Neuk.

Correct.

What disease does your father have?

MS.

I need the full name please.

Multiple sclerosis.

Correct.
What does multiple sclerosis mean?

Multiple sclerosis describes a medical syndrome in which the patient suffers a succession of attacks to their nervous system. These events are called sclerotic attacks. If you've had more than one attack you have multiple sclerosis.

Correct.

What causes a sclerotic attack?

It's a failure of the immune system. Basically the body starts attacking itself.

Wow.
Sounds weird.

It's pretty common.

Does anybody understand it?

Not really, no.

What sort of things can happen?

Legs go numb, eyes lose sight, pins and needles, hand tremors.

Is there anything you can do to control it?

Some people find that smoking marijuana helps to control the hand tremors.

Is your dad one of those people?

He is . . . although to be fair he liked a spliff before the whole MS thing happened so it's difficult to tell if he just uses it as an excuse.

Correct.
What's the outlook for a person with MS?

It depends. With each attack the body's ability to recover erodes and damage accretes. With each attack probablility of another attack increases.

That is incorrect.

Over time the patient becomes increasingly disabled and reliant on other people to –

I need the answer on the card.

– reliant on other people to help them.

That is incorrect.

As the person's condition degenerates –

LA LA LA LA LA LA LA LA –

– there is less time between recoveries.

LA LA LA LA LA LA LA –

Patients can end up in a wheelchair.

Buzzer noise.

I've started so I'll finish.
What is the outlook for a person with MS?

Everything will be completely fine as long as you don't think about it.

Correct.

*

Princess Duck looked out of the window and thought: that's just it, it's the thinking that's the problem. Normal people don't have to think about their lives. They just get on and live them. I have to think – all the time about everything. All these other castles, all these other kingdoms full of normal royal families. But not mine, thought Princess Duck, every spare inch of my head's filled with thoughts like a big cloud of biting cleggs on a hot day. 'What about the money?' 'How do you clean chocolate off a carpet?' 'What will the neighbouring lords say if they hear him crying?' And now . . .

Now with the sun filling the sky like the headlamp of a giant celestial chariot

Now she had to think about this:

How can a blind man cook a macaroni cheese?

*

Pretend.

How will that work?

Do you see my hand?

No.

Say yes.

Yes.

That's how it works.

Why don't you make lunch?

It has to be you.

Why?

If she thinks you can't look after me she'll take me away.

Maybe that would be best.

How?

Duck, I'm blind.

Temporarily. Optic neuritis. It's on the internet. It lasts a couple of weeks then everything goes back to normal. You knew it could happen. We can do this. We're a team.

We're a team.

Right, so what's your signature dish?

Leftover pizza.

Something cooked.

Chips?

You've seen the leaflets. It's all about five-a-day. Healthy eating. Home cooking. Seasonal produce.

OK.

What do you cook if you want to impress a lady?

Ham baps.

Ham baps?

Rosie used to love ham baps. If we were going on a trip I would make up a big bag of ham baps – floury rolls, slices of ham and cheese, tomato ketchup and a pinch of salt – wash it all down with half a bottle of Newcastle Brown Ale on the side of the road at the Spittal of Glenshee . . . Heaven.

We're not giving her ham baps.

Think! There must be something you can cook.

Macaroni cheese.

OK.
Good.
How d'you do macaroni cheese?

Cook the macaroni.

OK.

Grate the cheese.

OK.

Mix it up.

OK.

Put it in a pie.

What?

Put it in a wee crusty pie.

Macaroni Cheese doesn't come in a wee crusty pie.

It does in Greggs.

Dad!

I've never cooked anything in my life before. I've never had need to. Cereal for breakfast. Greggs for lunch. Pizza for tea. What's wrong with that? Why can't she just see us being normal?

Because normal for us is not normal for other people. We're weird.

I'm sorry. I can't do it.

You can.

How?

We just have to practise.

*

I don't know when I began this – writing – making stuff up. I think it started when I was ten – I was watching TV.

Duck.

Yeah?

I've got something for you.
A present.
I found it in WH Smiths'.

It's not my birthday.

Doesn't have to be your birthday to give you a present, does it?

What is it?

A book.

It's empty.

It's got a rose on it.
A rose is for Rosie.
I thought whenever you got the feeling you wanted to talk to her you could write in it.

It's got a lock.

So you can put your secrets in it too.

And that night I opened the book.

And that night I wrote.

*

The great hall of the castle was damp for it was a winter's
morn and the mists off of the great despondent sea hung
in the air and a scattering of dew lay over the tapestries
of naked ladies on motorbikes that lined the beast's hall.
He reached deep into the folds of his beastly raiment and
from outwith he drew forth a great leather book locked
with a key and he gave the book to the Princess Duck
and she saw that on the cover was a picture of a rose,
and the princess opened it and she saw the most beautiful
sight she had ever seen.

Fields upon fields upon fields of white.

Page after page of the most glorious empty blankness
stretching into the far distance, white fields just waiting
for her to run in them . . .

Thanks.

She kissed the beast and the beast smiled. He sank back
into the vastness of his cold stone throne and picked up
the stone remote control and pressed on its carved grid
and henceforth a band of travelling jesters appeared in
front of him and one of the jesters was called Clarkson
and he did perform amusing tales about chariots and the
beast called for ale and pies and his pipe and he did sit
and eat upon the ale and pies and laugh at the amusing
antics of the jesters until late into eventide.

*

We just have to practise.
Up to cupboard.
  Macaroni.
Open the bag.
Take it slowly.
Can't find tap.
  Ask your daughter.
  Just to the left.
Put the water on the boil.
  Next we fetch the olive oil.
Can't set the clock.
  I can, ten minutes.
I'm totally tragic.
Duck does all electric gadgets.
  Perfect.
Cheese in the fridge.
  Parmesan.
Everything is going to plan.
Grate it up.
  Watch your finger.
Now it's time for Dad to linger
While we wait to boil the water
Merry Christian chat with daughter
Blah blah blah church.
  Blah blah blah God.

Beep beep beep.

Drain the pan into the sink.

   Whoa!

Macaroni in the bowl I think.

Add the cheese.

   Mix it round.

Making food is fun I've found.

   Slice tomato

One two three.

Lay atop the macaronee.

Lastly with a little flourish

   Sprinkle herbs

Our health to nourish

   Fresh from garden.

No, they're not.

   Just say they are

   She'll like that a lot.

Now, how do I know the table's ready?

     I'll bang it once.

You know what, this scam might fly.

Dad's home-made macaroni pie.

   Put the dish down on the table.

Now if I judge it I should be able . . .

   If in doubt, Dad, ask for Duck.

OK –

Trips.

Owww.

Dad!

Sound of smashed dish.

Bollocks fuck!

OK, it's OK, it's fine. It was a triumph. We just need to watch what we're doing at the end. We've got ages before she comes.

Doorbell rings.

It's too early.

Look through the spy-hole and see who it is.

Duck peers.

Oh.

*

> Lawrence Lofthouse
> The most beautiful boy in the school
> He's the boy all the girls think is cool
> He's smooth as a smoothy
> He's as peachy as a peach
> He's right out of my league
> He's completely out of reach.

*

Who is it?

Nobody.
Somebody

I don't know.
A person.
A boy.
A friend.

A boyfriend?

No!

Right.

It's Lawrence Lofthouse.
The boy I sit next to in drama class.
We're doing a show together.
That's all.

Lawrence Hello . . . hello?

Well?

What?

Aren't you going to let him in?

Door opens.

Hey.

Slight swoon.

You took your time.

Sorry, I was just –

Can I come in?

No.

Oh? The thing is, I need to talk to you. It's important.
And it's quite personal.

Personal?

Yes.

Personal to me?

Yes.

Slight swoon.

. . .

Give me a minute.

Door slams.

He wants to come in.

*

Tell us, how d'ya meet him?

Oh, we're just working on a show together.

What kind of show?

It's about a girl group and their struggles to get to the top. I'm doing the script. Lawrence is designing the costumes.

Tell us, do you fancy him?

No.

Oh really.

He's interesting but I just like him as a friend, you know.

Yes, we see.

. . .

Of course
If you did fancy him
It would be totally understandable.

Well I suppose. I do fancy him just a little bit.

Just a little bit.

A tiny bit.

Awww.

I have this dream.

Tell us.
Tell us about your dream.

We're sitting together in class one day and I'm just looking at the way he's rolled up the sleeve of his school shirt, just oh so casually, and there's his arm and the freckles on it looking just heartbreaking and so I take off my glasses and I shake my hair and he looks round and he's

A blur

Surprised
Because he's seen that I was beautiful but in a way that had been hitherto completely unnoticeable.

He can't stop looking at me but I ignore him. I concentrate on writing our show. But can feel his hot gaze on me and I know he's thinking . . .

If only I weren't gay.

What?

Gay as a goose.

No.

Everybody knows that.

He never told me.

Why should he have to tell you every detail about his sexuality?

Pervert.

Just cos you're obsessed with him.

I'm not obsessed.

*

37

Lawrence DUCK? DUCK?

Dad – you've got *one minute* to help me tidy up.

*

Music from Benny Hill.

Pizza box?

Bin.

Pizza box?

Bin.

Pizza box?

Bin.

Bin's full.

Empty bin.

Bag's broke.

Balls.

Ugh.
You're not helping

I'm tidying.

You're just smearing the chaos around.

Sorry.

Lawrence DUCK!

Shove it in the cupboard.

Underpants?

In my pocket.

More pants?

In the oven.

Spliffy ashtray?

In the baked-bean tin.

Baked-bean tin?

In the cupboard

Bounty bars?

Bread bin.

More?

All done.

Great.

Wait.

What?

Something's wrong.

What?

You.

Me?

Get in the cupboard.

What?

You're don't look right.

Why?

Your T-shirt's got a curry stain
Your jeans are way too big for you
You haven't shaved.
Please, Dad, please.

Can't I go in my bedroom?

There isn't time.

Cupboard door slams.

*

Lawrence DUCK?

Door opens.

Hey.

Hey.

Where's your dad?

Out.

Will he be back?

Not for ages.

. . .

Duck, there's something I want to ask you.

Oh.

Something important.

Fire away.

Duck, ever since we've been sitting together in drama
class I've noticed you.
And . . .
Well . . .
Especially since working on this show with you –

Yeah?

There's something I've been thinking –

What?

It's a bit embarrassing.

Don't be embarrassed.

It's . . .

It's . . .

Say.

Duck –

Yeah?

Would you be willing to give me a public blowjob to help me prove I'm not gay?

*

It's not like I had crazy expectations. I wasn't expecting him to come in and say he loved me. I just thought for a second I might have a chance at a normal boyfriend, a boy where you can look at the back of his hands for a bit, a boy where you have that moment where you're both nearly nearly nearly touching for a bit. Call me old-fashioned but I just think it's a bit soon for . . . public blowjobs.

Plink plunk plonk.

Oh, get lost you –

You would like a visit from the Fairy of Normality.

I would.

Unfortunately she is not your fairy.

Tell me about it.

I am your fairy.
On the day you were born you were given me, and I was given you.
You cannot get rid of me.
You must accept me.
Stand on the edge of the cliff

Fall backwards into the darkness.
Give in to me.
Give in.

I will not.

I will not fall.

*

Motorcycle skid.

No no no no no no no!

Motorcycle crash.

*

You want me to WHAT?

Not a real blowjob. Just a pretend one. Tonight, at half
past six, behind the wall near the chippie. It needs to
be very noisy so people hear. And then – when people see
us – we'll pretend to be embarrassed about being caught.

Pretend?

You're good at that, Duck. That's what I noticed – in
drama class – when we've been working on our show.
You're brilliant at improvising. You have a talent. You're
definitely the best person to pretend to give me a blowjob.

But Lawrence, why?

Nobody takes me seriously. Alicia Coulter won't even
consider going out with me because she thinks I'm gay.

Aren't you?

No. I just like designing costumes.

Can't you tell people?

I've tried. But whenever I say anything about it people say, 'Ah methinks the lady doth protest too much.' Everybody's seen *Queer Eye for the Straight Guy* and Gok Wan and *Colin and Justin* and so folk think they know everything about gay people. Everyone's got a gaydar now. No, I've thought about it very carefully. The only way I stand a chance with Alicia Coulter is that I need to get caught doing something completely heterosexual – like, for example, getting a blowie off of you.

Well look – you'd be shooting yourself in the foot. If you get caught with me behind the chippie wall – yes that might suggest that you're not gay, but Alicia Coulter will just think you're going out with me?

Exactly, but this is part of my plan, if Alicia sees another woman giving me attention that will cause her to be sensitive to the competition and therefore it will increase her sexual interest in me.

Her sexual interest?

Yes.

Which is currently what?

Zero – to be fair.

It's all right to be gay – Lawrence.

I know that.

Actually it's great.

I know.

It's brilliant to be gay.

I totally accept that it's brilliant to be gay.

You should be proud of what you are.

I am – I am proud of what I am – I'm a straight man with an eye for good design.

OK?

OK.

Are you sure?

One thousand per cent certain.

OK.

OK.

You don't believe me.

No. I do.

You don't.

I do.

You see? You see why I have to do this? No matter what I do, people just make their own assumptions. Now are you going to help me or not?

*

> Think! Think!
> About your reputation
> Think! Think!
> Of what your friends will say
> Think about whether it's right to give a blowjob
> To a boy just in order to prove he's not gay!
> Just think
> Think
> Think!

*

No.

No?

Lawrence. I have some integrity. I am not for hire.

That's a shame.

Sorry.

I suppose I'll just have to take this bag of grass back to Vinnie.

What bag of grass?

This one.

That's my dad's.

No it isn't. I bought it.

What?

Vinnie's my cousin.
He told me your dad hasn't paid for his medication for nearly a month.

What?

He owes Vinnie over two hundred quid. He said something to Vinnie about surprisingly high internet bills.

No.

I thought if you were doing me a favour I'd do a favour for you but still – if you don't want it . . . ?

*

A lit match.
A joint.

I feel like I'm getting better. Today's bad because of the eyesight thing but I'm steady on my feet and that's not true some mornings. And I'm holding the coffee all right, aren't I? Still as a lake. It helps to smoke a joint. I feel like I'm getting better and if that carries on I can start to

45

do things again. If I can keep the hand steady I can start to put nuts and bolts together – I just need to get it so that I'm relaxed enough to work with the tiny wee screws – then when I get my sight back I'll get back to doing some repairing – Gary's always said I could go back to work when I'm feeling better and Gary's a prick but he's an honest prick. I'm sure he'd give me work if I asked him. Wouldn't take long to save up a couple of grand and then when my fingers are really back in the groove I'll get the monster in the hall fixed up. I'll fix her up and get her running smooth, then Duck and me – we'll pack a tent and a passport and we'll just take off. We'll drive down to Hull, we'll get ourselves on that ferry and when we get to Amsterdam we'll load up with some high-grade medicinal marijuana and head south: Belgium France Spain Italy. Just like me and Rosie did. Just Duck and me and the bike, I reckon we can make the trip last a couple of years and then . . . when things get bad, we'll drive to Switzerland.

Switzerland?

Switzerland, like at the end of *The Great Escape* . . . when Steve McQueen turns and he looks at the Nazis and he revs the bike, he lets go and he jumps right out into the air.

Sounds great.

Yeah.

'Born to Be Wild'.

Yeah.

Just like *Easy Rider.*

Have you seen that film?

Fifteen times.

I love that film.

Me too.

Have you seen that film, Duck?

No.

Lawrence has.

Good for Lawrence.

Mr Macatarsney.

Yes.

What is the monster in the hall?

*

The monster in the hall
Is clearly a metaphor
For the things in our lives we can't face

But It's also a real monster
And it's also a real hall
As Lawrence Lofthouse is about to find out.

*

Oh . . .
Oh . . .
Oh my God.

Yeah.

A Ducati Monster 796 series.

You know it?

Know it? Mr Macatarsney, this is the most beautiful
object I've seen in my entire life.

Isn't it just?

Scarlet and chrome.

It belonged to Rosie. I'm just in the final stages of restoration. It got pretty badly damaged in the accident.

Dad, you've been in the final stages of restoration for years.

These things take time.

I'm putting it in the cupboard.

A bike like that doesn't belong in a cupboard. A bike like that belongs on the hill roads of Italy . . . It's a design classic.

Unfortunately Duck doesn't appreciate it.

I do appreciate it, Dad, I just don't want the lady to think she's walked into a garage.

You should take a leaf out of Lawrence's book.

Should I?

Lawrence has an appreciation of the power of the imagination.

He certainly does.

Now . . . suit.

Suit?

You need to put your suit on.

I haven't got a suit.

You do.

Where?

Here.

She gives him the suit.

Mr Macatarsney, for a man with such a fine eye for Italian design you're a great disappointment when it comes to formal wear.

What?

Duck, that suit needs ironed.

I haven't got time.

I'll do it.
I can't bear to see clothing badly maintained.
. . .

Thanks.

*

Boys boys boys
Boys boys boys
It's often confusing when they're nice.

Sometimes it would be easier
If they were always bastards
At least that way you'd know where you were.

*

There's one last thing.

What?

Shh . . .

Why are you whispering?

I need your password.

Why?

Porn. The lady's bound to check it. She'll be trained.

49

That'll be something on her list. When we're not looking.
She'll switch it on and she'll rootle about and she'll find
all the I-don't-want-to-know. I need your password to
delete it all now.

Duck, there is no porn.

It's OK.
You don't need to pretend.
I'm not that innocent.

There isn't any porn – I swear.

Dad, when I go to bed you take a can of beer and a spliff
and a family pack of Bounty bars and sit up till three in
the morning. You're not telling me you're playing angry
birds.

No, but –

Just give me your password and I'll reset the browser and
it'll all be gone.

No.

It's not animals is it?

No!
For goodness sake.
Duck.
It's not porn.

What is it, then?

Otherworld.

Otherworld?

It's an MPU – a multiplayer universe – a game – a world –
a whole world on the computer. You create an avatar – a
character – and through your character you explore –
you go on adventures – fight monsters. Hunt for treasure
– collect magical weapons.

50

Collect magical weapons?

Yes.

That's what keeps you awake at night?

Yes.

You're weird.

Computer switch-on noise.

How do I log in?

Password's 'Voldemort'.
See – that first screen –

Yeah.

That's me.

Duke 101 – six-foot seven inches tall – strength: twenty –
steed: a gryphon – magic weapons: the Sword of
Gefolnirol – points:

21,467.

Is that good?

Pretty good.

Who's this?

What?

There's a woman standing beside you – I mean standing
beside the Duke?

Mistress Selkie.

I knew it.

What?

Porn.

No.

Don't be ridiculous.
She's just a friend.
She's my adventuring partner.

She has a bra with machine guns on it.

That's her avatar.
Avatars wear that sort of thing.
My avatar's wearing a loincloth,
Look –

NO!

It's fun, Duck. There's not much left I can do for fun at the moment, is there? I can't ride the bike. I can't drink. I can't go out with the Bad Boys. What's wrong with me spending a few hours on Otherworld every night?

She might be a man.

So?

It's not normal.

Duck, what is this obsession you're getting with being normal?

Dad – please!

   Doorbell rings.

Too late.

Mr Macatarsney, here's your suit. I've done my best with the shirt, but I can't work miracles with polyester.

Lawrence – get in the cupboard.

What?

I don't want the lady to see you.

What's wrong with me?

You're a boy.

I don't want to go in a cupboard.

Lawrence – if you want me to see you at the chippie later, do as I say. Or would you prefer me to tell everyone in school about your passion for menswear?

OK.

Cupboard door shut. From inside the cupboard:

I'm afraid of the dark.

Tough.
Let's get this over with.
OK. A visit from the Social Services.

*

Door.

Hello.

Hello.

You don't know me.

No.

I'm here because –

It's OK,
We know.
We've been expecting you.

Really?

Yes.

Good.
Can I come in?

Of course.
Dad!
The lady's here.

Can I introduce you to my father?
Dad this is – Mrs –

Agnetha.

Hugh.

When I stood at the door. I was afraid. I didn't know if you would invite me in and kiss me or maybe just tell me to fuck off.

Oh . . . no . . . we wouldn't do that.

I know.
Look at you.
Look at him.
Like a great bear – rising out of the tundra – roaring.
Just how I imagined.

    She roars.

Can I hug you – bear?

Goodness.

You're shaking.

Am I?

Just a little.

I didn't notice.

Are you hungover?

No.

Have you been drinking the darkness away, big bear?

Dad doesn't drink.

It's just a very mild symptom of the MS.

I didn't know you had MS.

He doesn't.

I don't?

No? It was a joke. Really he's just cold. Dad, put the heating on – he's a terrible one for sensible money management. It's just typical of the way we cope.

Agnetha?

Yes.

You don't sound like you're from Kirkcaldy, Agnetha.

I'm not. I'm from Trondheim. I just came over this morning. When I got on the plane I felt like slitting my wrists. You know how it is. Sometimes you see the faces of other human beings and you feel like jeesus we're all just so much flesh – so much animated wet flesh just smearing ourselves over this beautiful world like horrible jam . . . you know . . . But then. I knew I was coming to see you. So that cheered me up. You look surprised.

Flying.

Yeah – it's shit. Fucks up the environment. But for something as important as this –

I think I just thought you would live nearby.

And you.
You must be Duck?

That's me.

I've heard so much about you.

Good, I hope.

Not all good.
Sometimes I hear about all the crazy shit you get up to.
Ha ha.
You kids think we grown-ups don't know – we know.

Do you?

55

Don't worry.
I'm on your side.
My son Bo's a computer hacker.
He was crazy crazy too when he was your age.

I wouldn't say Duck was crazy crazy –

Duck – it's a funny name.

Short for Ducati.

Ducati was her mother's favourite motorbike.

Mindblowing. Awesome. I've seen a couple of Ducatis in my time but I've never ridden one. I'm not surprised she liked them. I'd love to feel one of those big bastards between my legs.

Right.

Broom-motherfucking-broom.

Sorry?

I ride a black Kawasaki on stage for my big entrances with the band. Lars pounds out a power chord and Erik starts up the solo – dry ice, and then I ride out on to the stage and sing –

You're in a band, Agnetha?

Yes.

What's its name?

Cuntblister.

*

Womaniscomingwomaniscomingsquealmalehellpig
womaniscoming.

*

It was Lars's idea. After I split up with Lars I got into anarcho-feminism and I wanted to change it to Cockblister but a lot of the fans have it tattooed on their arms now so they'd never forgive me if we changed it –

Agnetha, I'm wondering . . . I'm imagining you're quite busy . . . so I'm wondering is there anything in particular you want to ask us?

No . . . well . . . not really
Now I'm here I think I'm just happy to be –
No questions.
You know?
This situation is weird enough without questions.
Yeah?

Yeah.

I think let's all just fucking be.

Right.

. . .

. . .

Actually I do have one question.

Yeah.

Is it OK if I crash on your sofa tonight?

*

I don't remember much about my mum. I was three when she died. I remember she was beautiful. Dad called her Beauty and he was The Beast. They met at the Isle of Man TT races. Rosie was racing. Everyone fancied Rosie because she looked good in leather but she was going out with a big fellow called Hartlepool Jack who was the size of three houses so nobody would even look at her in case he knocked them over. But on this particular day at the TT races Rosie rode a blinder and she beat all the men in the race, she even beat Hartlepool Jack, and when she got off the bike at the end and went to collect the trophy Jack shoved her – just pushed her over into the dust, and he said she was never ever to humiliate him like that again. Rosie picked up a bottle of Newcastle Brown Ale, smashed it over the back of a nearby Harley and dived at Hartlepool Jack's face. Just as she was in mid-air Dad saw his chance. He pushed Jack out of the way and took the bottle himself – a stab in the leathers – not because he wanted to save Jack but because he wanted to save Rosie. Dad took the hit so that Rosie could be saved from jail. When Rosie calmed down she apologised to him. He said it was nothing. She bought him a drink.

'Great race today.'
'Yeah.'
'You passed me on the hill – I couldn't see you for dust.'
'I was flying.'
'You looked like you were chasing something.'
'More like running away.'

And then they looked at each other and the sun went down and drew a shimmering purple line across the grey of the Irish Sea and silhouetted the two of them.

Dad was the first man Rosie had found who didn't want to be faster than her and she was the first woman he'd found who wanted looking after with the same care he looked after his bikes. That night they realised they would be together for ever – if he survived that is – because while they'd been talking he'd been bleeding under his leathers from the open wound of her stab and even though he'd felt dizzy and sick with a warm wet feeling round his stomach he'd put that down to falling in love which was something he'd never done before so he suddenly sighed and fell back in a dead faint and his eyes rolled back in his head and Mum strapped him to the back of her bike and she rode over the mountains to the clinic in Peel. She got him there just in time. The doctor said five minutes later and he'd have died.

To this day

Hugh Macatarsney still says:

Duck,

If someone tells you they think they're falling in love,

Check for a stab wound,

Just in case.

*

Selkie. You're Mistress Selkie.

Of course. Who else did you think I was?

It doesn't matter.

Selkie?

How did you find me?

Oh, it was easy. Bo traced your IP address so I knew you lived somewhere round here. I figured if fate wanted us to meet – fate would make it happen. I took the plane and the bus and the train and when I arrived in your town pretty much the first thing I saw was a sign saying – Duke's Motorcycles 101 High Street – Duke 101. I went in and asked for Duke. They told me where you were. Fate.

Agnetha, why are you stalking my dad?

To talk about what happened on the moors of Belorno.

Oh.

Yes.

What happened in the moors of Belorno?

. . .

WHAT HAPPENED ON THE MOORS OF BELORNO?!

I asked her to marry me.

*

Why's the sky purple?

The fires of Tarsus,

They keep changing colour.

It's beautiful.

What planet is this?

Belorno.
The tower's towards the east-north-east.

My gryphon's dead.
We'll have to walk.

Is that smoke?

It's mist on the moor?

The moor looks silver in the double moonlight.

Beautiful.

Somewhere out there hides the Chimaera.

We're strong.

We could die tonight.

I know.

We have adventured together long.

Yes.

Duke, if one of us dies we might never find the other one again.

Neither of us will die.

I know.
Still.
I'm scared.

Scared?
But you have 32,000 kill points.
And machine-gun breasts.
What have you got to be scared of?

You.

Me?

Duke,
I have feelings for you.

Duke?

I have feelings for you too.

Action Option 4 kiss: romantic.

Kiss.

Kiss.

Kiss.

Kiss.

Selkie?

Yes.

What's that coming out of the fires of Tarsus?

Chimaera!

Chimaera attacks from sky.

Selkie turns.

Duke spins.

Selkie raises lance.

Duke prepares firespell.

Selkie spins left.

Chimaera spins left.

Firespell catches Chimaera.

Chimaera's wings burnt.

Selkie fires machine-gun breasts.

Chimaera hit.

Chimaera falls.

Duke raises lance.

Lance impales Chimaera.

Firespell.

Chimaera burns.

Selkie raises fist.
Yes.

Chimaera dead.

I tell you what we need –
We need lager.

Why?

To go with our late-night kebab.

Selkie laughs out loud.

Duke laughs out loud.

*

Princess Duck stared out of her tower at the great grey waste of the despondent sea and saw the black sails of the ship of the Queen of Norway parked in the harbour like a bad memory.

Far away in the cold stone hall she could hear them sitting on his cold stone throne drinking mead and laughing and talking about their adventures in the other world.

I hate queens, Duck thought.

If they're not coming to take you away then they're coming to take away your father.

*

From the cupboard:

Duck.

Yes.

Can I come out of the cupboard now?

No.

You have a boy in the cupboard?

Yes.

Is he your boyfriend?

Sort of.

Duck, you truly are a death-metal feminist chick. You raawk.

No. No, I don't raawk and I'm not any kind of a chick. Do you understand? I'm normal. I'm a normal girl and this is my normal dad and . . . and you're weird.

Duck –

No – listen to me, Dad – this woman is not real. You don't know her. She doesn't know you. She has a nose ring. For all you know she could be a bloodthirsty murdering maniac.

She is a bloodthirsty murdering maniac, that's why I like her.

You know what I mean.

No I don't. I don't know what you mean.

I mean that you and her – you think you know each other, but you don't. You're total strangers. You just know each other's typing.

That's not fair.

You don't know anything about my father.

I know he's kind.
I know he's loyal
And trustworthy
And funny
And

And?

I know he loves me.

Oh you know that. Do you?

Yes.

Do you know that he's blind? You didn't know he had MS. Do you know that whenever it is you're wandering through the wilderness of Bumclencho with your magic swords in your hand he's sitting up here in a dark damp wee room smoking dope to keep his hand from shaking and eating Bounty bars to stave away the munchies? And do you know that when he gets up to go to the toilet he wobbles because his whole left leg's frozen because it

64

hasn't recovered from the last attack and even though he won't admit it he can't stand up properly so he wobbles down the corridor dropping chocolate bars which he can't pick up and when he tries to pee he can't stand still so he misses the toilet and he can't bend down so he tries to wipe it up with his sock? And do you know that when he's finished swearing and cursing and he wobbles back down the hall to join you in Lalaland, and I get up and I get a mop from the cupboard and I clean up after him. And I do it all really really quietly because I don't want him to know. Did you know that?

I didn't think so. You don't know my father and you don't know me and you've got no business being here.

Maybe I'd better go?

Agnetha . . .

You better had. Get out before I throw you out.

The doorbell rings.

Shit.

We haven't got time.

Agnetha. In the cupboard now.

Door opens.

Hey Duke!
There's a monster in here.

Yeah.

Can I sit on it?

Be my guest.

Door.

From the cupboard:

Broom-motherfucking-broom.

Duck – that was way out of order.

Was it?

You've got no right to interfere like that.

You're my dad.

The doorbell rings again.

We haven't got time for this now.

I'll get the door.
You stand by the living-room table.
When she comes in
Reach out
'Pleased to meet you'
Shake hand
Sit.
Got it?

Got it.
Reach out
'Pleased to meet you'
Shake hand
Sit.

Door opens.

Hello.

Hello.

He reaches out his hand.

Pleased to meet you.

Shakes hand.
Sits.
Misses the chair.
Glass smashing.

Ahh!

Dad!

What?

I think I've sat on the bong.

*

Computer game bad noise.

Life's a game of Tetris and it's just gone up a level.

*

Level One.

Level set-up noise.

> Not to worry.

> So, my name's Linda Underhill and really I'm just here to get a sense of how you're getting on and to see whether there's more we could be doing to help you.

Great

> Super

> So how are you getting on?

We're getting on great.

> We're getting on super.

> Good.

> Perhaps we'll just start with you filling out these forms for me.

Computer game bad noise.

Forms?

> Nothing to worry about, just a few basic
> questions to help us get a sense of income and
> benefits, child tax credits and so on that you're
> claiming so we can see if there's any discrepancies
> with what you might be entitled to.

Right.

> Do you need a pen?
> Do you need a pen?
> Mr Macatarsney?

The thing is, Mrs Underhill . . . I'm

> A gardener.

> Oh?

And we planned to show you the garden.

Yes.

> We grow our own vegetables.

> That's nice.

You really should see them.

> Maybe after lunch.

While the sun's out.

> Actually it looks a little damp out there.

Damp? It's roasting.

> My kagoul's out on my moped.

Dad's really proud of his garden.

> . . .
> . . .
> I'll get my kagoul.

Computer game good noise.

*

Level Two.

   Level set-up noise.

   Cupboard door opens.

Agnetha!

I need your help.
I'm going to take the lady into the garden.
I need you to help Dad fill out this form.
Will you do it?

OK.

Great.

The light, the light, I need the light.

What happened to Lawrence?

Panic attack.
I had to stun him.
An old Taekwondo trick I picked up from the women's refuge.
He's breathing but he'll stay quiet.

Good work.

   Computer game good noise.

*

Level Three.

   Level set-up noise.

   Thunder, rain.

It's just haar.
Glorified mist.

Big thunder. Big rain.

What do you grow?

Grass.
Grass mainly.
Edible grass.
And nettles.

Well – you've certainly got a healthy crop of
nettles.

Yes.

Growing out of the sofa.

. . .
And brambles.
And a fridge.

Thunder and rain.

Shall we go in?

Computer game good noise.

*

Level Four.

Level set-up noise.

Let's see then, 'Benefits Claimed' – you've ticked
incapacity benefit, child tax credits – free
prescriptions – that's due to the MS. I take it –
child benefit – I notice you've written here – 'free
helicopters on demand'?

Computer game bad noise.

Did I write that?

That's what's down here.

Pen must have slipped.

By 'Income' you've written: 'Property is theft. We demand real existing Socialism. From each according to his abilities, to each according to his needs.'

Computer game bad noise.

Dad!

'Marital Status': None –
'Love is free. Love has no chains. Throw off the yoke of patriarchy now! We demand rebel sex.'

Computer game bad noise.

'Reclaim your lives from the death system of war and oil and cry anarchy anarchy anarchy for ever!'

Computer game bad noise.

And you've drawn a big A in a circle all over the form.

I can explain.

I know the forms can be frustrating but –

Dad's such a joker.
Why don't you leave them with me and I'll type them out properly on the computer?

Good idea.

If it's all right, can I just take a look round the house?

Fine.

Computer game good noise.

*

Level Five.

Level set-up noise.

Duke does a short version of the dance of lunch.

> To the cupboard
> Macaroni
> Open bag
> Take it slowly
> Get the pan
> Fill with water
> Turn the tap
> Chat with daughter.

Mrs Underhill coughs.

> Mr Macatarsney?

Ho!

> Sorry.

Didn't know you were there.

Computer game bad noise.

> I've had a look round.
> Everything seems in order.
> Lots of books.

Yeah.

> Good to see you creating an environment of
> learning.

Oh that's not me.
That's Duck.
Duck loves books.
Stories.
She wants to be a writer.

> Does she?

She's completely passionate about it.

> Good.
> That's great.

Computer game good noise.

*

Level Six.

> *Level set-up noise.*

>> Well, I've looked at the forms
>> They seem great.
>> May I use your toilet?

Certainly.

>> Where is it?

Just through there.

>> Thanks.

> Dad!

What?

> That isn't the toilet that's the –

Mrs Underhill screams.

A door slams.

> Cupboard.

Computer game bad noise.

>> I opened the door and – a face –
>> Horrible
>> Her eyes were wide and she
>> Loomed at me –

Loomed?

> Covered in metal piercings – eyes all black – hair
> all red and she was cradling a dead boy!

Ohh . . . That –

That's

> You remember, Dad.

Yes, I remember.

> The looming face

It's my –

> His –

Sex doll.

> No!

No.

> Art.

It's my art.

> Your art?

I sculpt. Duck's a writer. I'm a sculptor. Right now I'm
sculpting the face of . . .

> A scary woman holding a dead boy on a
> motorbike.

It's a project.

> It's about grief.

We keep it in the cupboard.

> That's why the face is sad.

> *Computer game good noise.*

I am so sorry. I totally understand.

Do you?

Many people we work with use art as a means to help them explore the feelings they have about their difficulties. It can be a great way to release trapped emotions. It was insensitive of me to scream. I had no right to call it horrible. Would you like me to look at it again?

No!

It's not finished.

Great.
So, Duck? The toilet?

Through there.

Thanks.

Computer game good noise.

We got away with that.

I've about OD'd on adrenaline, Duck.
I can't take much more of this.

Hang in there, Dad. We're nearly done.

Toilet flush.

Shit!

What?

I totally forgot to mop up the wee after last night.

Computer game bad noise.

Mrs Underhill –

Trousers bit wet –

Burst pipe –

I'll get the council to send a plumber.

Computer game good noise.

*

Level Seven.

Level set-up noise.

Crowd noise – a stadium.

A commentator for the game.

   Welcome to Level Eight.

   Let's watch Duck and the Duke make lunch.
   It's a tough one – can they cope?

 Ready?

As I'll ever be.

   Let's do lunch!

Open the cupboard.

Macaroni.

 Clatter.

   And a bin bag's fallen on her head.

  Aaargh. Ohhh.

 Other cupboard.

Righty ho.

 Sorry.

   No you're fine.

And again.
Macaroni.

Dad!

  That's a baked-bean tin full of spliff ends.

Pour in pan.

  It's gone all over Underhill.

I'll just wipe it.

  No you're OK.

Turn the tap
And
Add the water

  Whhooaa!

  And he's missed the pan.

Ooops.

  I'll get a towel

  It's only water

   Nice to see the water mixing with the spliff
   ash making a kind of clay paste there.

  It'll come out in the wash.

Pan on the boil.

AAAAAARGH!

  Hand on the hob.

Aaaaaaarghhhhghha agh agh!

  Are you all right?

 In pain.

Fine.

  Are you sure?

Flesh wound.

    Pain.

Grate the cheese.

       Parmesan.

          Are you sure you're OK?

This is my signature dish, you know.

          Really?

Really.

Aahhhhhhhhh!

          He's grated his own knuckles.

    Pain.

          Oh dear oh dear oh dear.

    Pain.

          Blood everywhere.

    I'll get a plaster.

          He's felt that

Where were we?
Oh yes.
Macaroni

          Nice move.
          Smooth.

In the oven.

          Opens it up and . . .
          That's a pair of pants.

    Don't need those!

          She's thrown them out the window.

Duck, set the clock, please.
I'm totally tragic –
Duck does all electric gadgets.

There.

How long?

Ten minutes.

Tick tick tick tick tick.

Great.

Great.

Great.

Remember that time we were in church,

Eating healthy food,

Having a pray?

Yeah.

Great.

Great.

Great.

Tick tick tick.

Bounty bar to keep you going?

I don't think so.

Beep beep beep beep.

Ready to go!

And

Owwwww!

He's forgotten it's going to be hot.

Glass smashing.

He's dropped it.

Bollocking
Arsing
Cocks

Macaroni all over the floor.

Pain.

It's fine.
I'll just pop it on the table.
Mrs Underhill doesn't mind a little bit of dirt,
Do you, Mrs Underhill?

No.

Pain.

She's lost it now.
He's crying.
She's just plopping handfuls of macaroni
down on the table as if she were making
mud pies.

Lovely.

There.

Herbs?

You're all right.

They're seasonal.

Not that pocket.

Oh no!
That's a bad one.
That's Lawrence's big bag of grass.

Sprinkle sprinkle sprinkle.
Lovely.

Computer game bad noise.
Computer game bad noise.
Computer game bad noise.

Game over.

*

Sometimes Princess Duck sat in her tower and wondered how it would be if she had had some other life. If she had been brought up in one of the normal castles. Would she be prettier? Would she be cleverer? Would she be happier? What sort of princess would she be? Sometimes she imagined her mother riding across the dark fields that stormy night and wondered what might have happened if the white horse hadn't risen to throw her.

Sometimes she wondered.

But the truth is

She would never know

Because Duck was born doomed.

She'd been thrown into the jousting ring on her own and while life was galloping towards her on a great black charger she'd been given a donkey and a blunt stick.

Princess Duck got ready to take another blow.

*

Thank you for that visit. It's really been super. I'll take these forms away and we'll see about your benefits. I think we should be able to work out some improvements to your situation. In the meantime, Duck, here's a couple of leaflets that give you an idea of some of the services for young people that you can access.

Leaflets?

Yes.

That's all.

Yes.
What did you expect?

Nothing.

Great.
Well, once again, super to see you.
Have a nice afternoon.
Thanks for lunch.
Goodbye.

Doorbell rings.

*

Cupboard door opens.

All dance and leap about and kiss.

Door opens.

Hello!

Cupboard door shuts.

Forgot my kagoul.

Door shuts.

Cupboard door opens.

Party.

Door opens.

Oh, one last thing –

Cupboard door shuts.

How old are you, Duck?

Sixteen.

Thought so.
Thanks.
Bye.

Door shuts.

Cupboard door opens.

Has she really gone this time?

Moped noise.

She's gone.

They party till they're pooped.

*

Keith.

Yes, David?

I think it's time.

Time for what, David?

I think it's time we heard a little bit more about a very special lady.

Who might that be, David?

I think it's time we told these good people about

Mrs Linda Underhill.

Wha wha wha oooh.

Come on, people.

Let's climb into the limousine of love

And let's drive down to Kirkcaldy.

Let's go down to the seafront where the cargo ships sit offshore

And let's pull up alongside Mrs Linda Underhill.

She's stopped at the traffic lights.

She's sitting on her moped in the rain.

Let's wind down our window of imagination

And let's say

Hello

Hello

Wah wah wah oooooh.

Mrs Linda Underhill is a social worker.

Social worker.

Every day she's invited into the lives of people who are teetering on the edge of catastophe.

Catastrophe.

And every day does her best to bring them back.

Back.

She likes to hold out a helping hand.

Helping hand.

You see – Mrs Linda Underhill knows that life is like a walk across a great frozen lake. Most of the time the ice is so thick you can drive trucks on it, build igloos on it, scoot about and slide. Most of the time most people going through life would never know there was a great dark lake beneath them.

But it's there.

It's always there –

And at any moment a crack can open up –

Crack –

You lose your job –

Crack –

You get cancer –

Crack –

There's a patch of oil on the road near the turn-off to Coaltown of Balgonie.

And when that crack opens up you start to fall,

The ice tips and you slide,

And you shout out,

But nobody seems to hear –

Well, that's where Mrs Linda Underhill comes in. She hears. She listens for the crack. She looks out for people who're sliding towards the black and she runs after them and tries to draw them back up from the edge.

Which she mostly does with leaflets.

Leaflets that describe courses. Leaflets that tell you about diseases. Leaflets for helplines. Leaflets that tell you where you can go if you're bisexual or lesbian or transgendered or gay.

She does an awful lot else, obviously, home visits and case conferences and –

But leaflets are important –

Yes.

Because those leaflets sit there in a person's house, like a kind of magic dust, just waiting for the moment when a person needs them. And when a person needs them.

They're there.

Mrs Linda Underhill sees herself as a sort of Fairy of Normality.

Patrolling the frozen lake of life on her moped, in her pink kagoul in the rain.

Why?

Because Mrs Linda Underhill has a philosophy.

Life isn't a competition. We don't win by defeating others. We all win together or we all lose. If we compete with each other . . . we all end up hurt. Time. Money. Love. Whatever the resource, the best thing is to share.

That's what Mrs Linda Underhill believes.

So –

Even though she is very tired –

Even though she has three more houses to visit today –

And even though the lights have turned green –

Mrs Linda Underhill is going to rev her moped's engine and turn around.

Because Mrs Linda Underhill can't stop thinking about Duck Macatarsney

And she's just remembered –

There's a really interesting leaflet that she's forgotten to deliver.

Wah wah wah oooooooh.

*

Now all Duck has to do is work out how to give a public blowjob to Lawrence Lofthouse behind the chippie wall.

I've written a script.

'Exterior, the chippie, day.'
Duck says 'Oh Lawrence.'

You don't say 'Duck says,'
That just tells you it's you.

Oh OK.
'Oh Lawrence I'm so horny.'

'We can't do anything about that here, Duck.'

'Oh please. I really want to have sex with you.'

'We can't have sex outside the chippie, Duck.'

'Why not?'

'Everyone will see.'

'Behind this wall, then. No one can see us there.'

OK – you're going to need to speak more loudly.

Loudly?

Otherwise they won't hear.

This is awful. The script doesn't make any sense.
The way you've written it I come across as a
nymphomaniac.

So?

That's not a brilliant plan if you want to persuade people
you're not gay. It should be you who wants sex. You
should be crazy for me.

Would that be believable?

What?

Well, with your look.

Jeans and a band T-shirt.
Glasses.
It's a bit – roadie.

Roadie?

I don't believe that I would fancy you dressed like that.

I don't believe I would say any of these lines.

Well, I'm the director.

Well, change your leading lady.

. . .

. . .

All right – you win, you have a look at the script, I'll
have a look at the costumes.

Fine.

*

OK – I've gone through your wardrobe and I've found
this. If you wear it with this belt and those shoes and
I pin it back here it just might work. Try it.

She does.

Take your glasses off.

She does.

Shake your hair.

She does.

Oh.

What?

Nothing.
Just
  . . .

Nothing.

You be Lawrence.

I'll be Duck.

'Duck.'

'Yes.'

'I want you. I can't keep quiet about it any more. In the drama class I sit beside you. I watch you breathing. I see your skin through the white of your shirt. I see the way your hair meets the nape of your neck and I want to touch you – I see the way you half smile as you write and I want you so much I feel it taking me over and I want to grab you –' This stuff's actually quite good. Duck –

OK, come closer, come in here like this, so we're next to each other.

OK.

And so then you look into my eyes.

Right.

Longingly.

OK.

And then you touch my face.

Right.

Lawrence,

Yes.

Something's throbbing.

Oh.
That's my phone.

*

Thunder. Rain.

Hello?
Hello again?
It's me – Linda Underhill? Sorry to bother you.
May I come in?

Of course.

Oh hello.

This is my – friend, Agnetha.

Hello, Agnetha.

Hello, Linda.

I saw you in the cupboard?

Yes. I was hiding.

We just thought it would be confusing if she was around when you were around.

It is.

Would you prefer it if I went back in the cupboard?

I think it might be easier.

OK.

No problem.

Cupboard door shuts.

Right.
That's better.

She's from Norway.

Mr Macatarsney.

Yes.

You're having problems with your vision, aren't you?

How did you know?

It's a known side effect of MS.
And you sat on a bong.

Oh.

The trouble is
You didn't mention it on your form.

No.

Why not?

Actually Agnetha wrote the form.

So she's the Socialist.

Anarchist.
Sorry.

No – don't be. I totally agree with everything she wrote.
It cheered me up in fact. 'From each according to their
ability, to each according to their need.'

Yes.

But that's just the thing, Mr Macatarsney, if you don't
put down your needs, then I can't get the council to try to
meet them.

The thing is. I'm worried that if I put down on that form
that I'm blind you're going to think we can't cope and
you're going to take Duck away.

Take her away?

Put her into care.

Oh no no. Care is always a last resort. Duck would have
to be in a far, far worse situation than she is now before
we'd even begin to consider drastic action like that.

   Phone rings.

Do you want me to get that?

No, It'll just be someone selling something.

On the answerphone:

Hi, we're not in, please leave a message after the beep.

Beep.

'Oh.'

'Oh.'

'Oh.'

'Oh Duck – oh my God – that feels so good.
Oh DUCK!'

And we're done.

Great.

So let's get this straight. Later this evening we'll do that
again behind the chippie wall where everyone can see us
and afterwards you'll give me a bag of grass. Yeah?

Beeeeeeeeeeeeeep.

Ah.

Ah.

*

What?

Something up with my phone.
I'll switch it off.

Weird, doing that.

Yeah.

Do you want to go over it again?

Maybe we should.

Maybe just one more time.

Do the bit where you take your glasses off and shake your hair.

OK.

   Duck does so.

Duck.

What?

You're beautiful.

Am I?

   They nearly kiss.

Lawrence.

. . .

Is this real or a rehearsal?

Real.

   They nearly kiss.

   Mrs Underhill coughs.

Whoahha!

I'm sorry to interrupt but – Duck – but I wondered if I could I have a word.

*

I can explain.

Duck – I wonder if it would help if you had a break.
A little bit of time away from home.
I've had an idea for a residential that I think might interest you.

I know it's a bit last minute but –
I've made all the arrangements.
Why don't you pack an overnight bag
And I'll tell you all about it.

Right.

I'll wait for you in the hall.

*

Duck throws the leaflet away.

Dad!

Duck?

Out the window.

What?

We're going to jump.

We're two floors up.

There's a sofa.

*

Aaaaaaaaaaaaaaaaarrgh –

Aaaaaaaaaaaaaaaaargh –

Ngmph.

*

Duck – is this the lady's moped?

Yes.
We're stealing it.

Why?

She's going to put me into care.

No, Duck, she's not.

She is. She asked me to pack an overnight bag.
I'm not going back.

Where are we going?

We're going to Europe.

Broom-motherfucking-broom.

Weedy motorcycle noise.

We don't have any money, Duck.

I'll earn us money.

How?

Writing.

What?

My novel. I'm nearly nearly finished it. It's about a
princess in a tower and she lives with a beast and . . .

You can't just write a novel.

J.K. Rowling did.

Stop the moped.

If she can do it, I can too.

DUCK, NO.

She stops the moped.

Duck, we've tried. But it won't work. You know and I
know that we can't go on like this. We have to give up.
I'm not looking after you any more. You're looking after
me and it's not working. We need help.

Get off the moped.

Duck.

TRAITOR!

Moped sound.

DUCK!
Duck.

Rain.
Thunder.

Duck.

*

Alone
Alone
By the side of a B-road
In the rain
Alone
That's what life is.

*

The sound of a motorcycle, its revs deep and loud.

Mr Macatarsney!
Mr Macatarsney!

Mrs Linda Underhill?

Hello!

How did you get here?

Well, when I explained the situation to your friend
Agnetha she pointed out that you had a motorbike in
your hall cupboard which she was pretty certain she
knew how to fix.

I know those babies like the back of my hand!

And Lawrence here was able to quickly adapt the various motorcycle leathers in your wardrobe so that they would fit us all.

You've actually got some super vintage stuff there, Mr Macatarsney.

Agnetha rode the bike down the stairs out the front door and we mounted in pursuit.

Damn, you're good.

Where's Duck?

She's gone.

What? Where?

That way?

Mr Macatarsney,
Climb on board.

Technically it's illegal to ride with four on a motorcycle but I think in this instance we can consider bending the law.

Anarchy!

Motorcycle revs.

There's a fork in the road!

One way says Milton of Balgonie.

The other says Coaltown of Balgonie.

Which way do you think she went?

That way.

Motorcycle roars away.

*

Traffic sound.

There she is.
Overtake.

Duck!

Moped sound.

Go away!

Duck!

Duck – it's me – Linda Underhill – I just wanted to give you this leaflet – and explain – nobody wants to put you into care – it's just that I saw that you were interested in creative writing and –

Watch out!

Massive truck goes past and toots its horn.

– creative writing, and I remembered that there's a group of kids –

She's getting away.

Left turn coming up.

Motorbike screech.

Where did she learn to ride like that?

She has her mother's wheels.

They meet every Wednesday, Duck, they're called Fife Young Carers –

LOOK OUT!

A lorry toots.

Fife Young Carers – Duck – and what they do is help you – get things – a bit more normal –

Steep downhill section.

She'll go out of control –

DUCK!

They're doing a residency in Dunfermline . . . for two nights. We'll organise some care at home for your dad.

I can't see in this rain.

Slow down, Duck, you crazy chick!

God, she looks good on a bike!

We're near the tree.
We must be near the tree.

Just a couple of nights away with kids in the same situation. Just a chance to learn about creative writing. Duck.

Sharp corner coming up.

Oh God.

Just a chance to see that you're not –

*

Alone! Alone!
Ultimately we're alone
On a moped on a B-road
In the rain.

My eyes full of tears
And nobody cares
I hope that I skid
And crash into a tree.

No one can stop her now.

Duck!

Motorcycle skid.

No no no no no no no!

Motorcycle crash.

*

Duck hits the tree.

Somewhere in the middle of a white field rides a girl in the mist and all she can see is white and grey and there seems to be no up and no down. It's over, she thinks. And her charger rears and throws her up, up into the white of the air and she falls –

Hanging like damp in the morning air –

Falls –

Slowly oh so slowly –

Down –

Not towards darkness.

But towards light.

Silence.

*

Duck, Duck, are you there, Duck?
Is that the wind or is that you breathing?
OK, look – you don't need to say anything but I'm going to try to walk towards you.
Will you warn me if I'm about to go over on a stone?
Will you?
OK, well, I'll just assume you will.
You took the corner too fast.
Same corner as your mum.
Is this the same tree?

I think it is.
The same one she hit.
I can feel the cut where her bike tore the bark.
Duck?
Duck?

*

Plink plunk plonk.

You again.

It is I, your Fairy Badmother.

What are you doing here?

I put a wee oil slick on the road back there.

Why can't you just leave me alone?

Because I care.

Care? I had just about got away from Social Services. I
nearly did it. If it hadn't been for you I'd have got away
with it. Lunch, Lawrence, the lady . . . I was on top of it
all. But every time I was about to win you stepped in and
screwed things up.

Someone had to stop you, Duck.

Why?

Shhh . . . Listen . . .

*

Your mother just loved being out in front. Not me, I'm
too scared. I give up when the road runs out, but Rosie
would carry on, faster and faster. The night she died we
were racing in the rain. I shouted out to her, 'I give up.
You win.' But she didn't hear over the engine and the rain

or maybe she didn't care because I don't think she was racing me anyway. She was racing against herself.

And a race against yourself – that's a race you're never going to win.

Sometimes, Duck, the way to win
Is to admit defeat.

It's too late.

No.

I'm lying dying under a tree. I can't go back now.

Why not?

It'd be embarrassing . . .

It's never too late, Duck.

A moment.

*

Duck opens her eyes.

Dad?

Duck?

They hug.

Poor Duck.
Your face is wet.
Is it rain? Or is it blood?

He tastes.

Rain.

Am I going to be OK?

Yes, I think so. Mopeds don't really go more than twenty-five miles an hour. I think you're probably just winded.

Oh.

. . .

That's a bit embarrassing.

Yeah.

Dad . . . I think I would like to read some of that lady's leaflets.

Yes.

Rain.

*

And so it was that when it was all over and the bruising was healed that one grey day Princess Duck kissed goodbye to Sir Lawrence who was now known throughout the kingdom as –

Sir Ladylover Lawrence –

On account of his going out with Princess Duck who was now known as –

Princess Swan –

on account of the astonishing makeover which Sir Ladylover Lawrence had brought to her daily look.

So Princess Duck-stroke-Swan kissed her knight goodbye and she joined with other princes and princesses from other weird castles in a caravan across the kingdom to the castle of the scribes in Dunfermline where she was to participate in a creative scroll-writing course presided over by a famous bard.

And in the cold stone hall of the cold stone castle the beast sat on his cold stone, cold stone throne and looked out at the great despondent sea that stretched grey all the way to the Queen of Norway's mountain homeland.

And the Queen of Norway said:

Maybe I shouldn't have come, big guy.

Why not?

I think maybe I screwed things up for you.

No.

It was supposed to be a nice surprise and – maybe, you know – fun.

I know, Agnetha, but look at me –

I'm a bald, middle-aged Scotsman in a wee house. A guy who can't keep his hands still long enough to light a fag. A blind guy. You don't belong with a guy like me. Go home. You've had a lucky escape.

You're lucky you can't see me.

Oh yeah.

Truth is, big guy, I look like a troll. A troll with a moustache. And my belly. You should see it. It's giant. Like a big behemoth. A hairy behemoth.

I don't believe you.

Touch me.

What?

Hold out your hand.

> *He holds out his hand.*
> *She guides it.*
> *He touches her face.*

You are a hairy behemoth.

I am.

A lovely hairy behemoth.

And you are a lovely beast.

Duke feels his chest.

What?

Just checking for stab wounds.

And just at that moment they kissed, which is something it's not necessary for us to see. And meanwhile far away in Dunfermline, the bard called forth Princess Duck-stroke-Swan and said to her:

OK, Duck, if you'd like to go first, why don't you read out what you've brought to the group . . . OK?

. . .

Duck?

. . .

Are you OK?

Coughs.

Is this on?

Testing –

Testing –

Testing –

1, 2, 3 –

Go!